ACKNOWLEDGMENT

Resurgence Books would like to acknowledge the talent of Chrissie Wright in the crafting of these children's materials. This series would not have been possible without her expertise in children's education and her discerning mind for sound, engaging, and age-appropriate theology.

Thank you, Chrissie.

Lost and Found Kids: 4/5/6 Workbook
Teaching God's Story from Creation to Kingdom Come

Published by Resurgence Publishing 1411 NW 50th Street

Seattle, WA 98107

First printing, 2012 Printed in the United States of America

ISBN-13: 978-1-938805-10-3

TABLE OF CONTENTS

STEWARDSHIP

KINGDOM

WHAT'S IN THIS BOOK?

This is the workbook four-, five-, and six-year-olds will use every week as you learn about new doctrines, and how they connect to God's Big Story with Jesus as Hero. Read on to find out what you will be doing each week to help you learn about who God is and who you are.

FOCUS ACTIVITY

This is what you will do when you enter your classroom. The Focus Activity will help get you ready for the day's lesson: it will either get you thinking about what you already know, or connect the day's Big Idea to some experiences in your own life.

ACTIVITY

This is what you will complete in your Community Group to help what you learned in the lesson stick in your brain.

SCRIPTURE EXPLORATION

This page will help you explore a verse in the Bible that connects to what you learned during the lesson. The goal here is to better understand pieces of Scripture—to explore, not memorize.

TRINITY: Lesson 1, Focus Activity

When you hear the word "beautiful," what do you think of? In the picture frame, draw as many things as you can.

TRINITY: Lesson 1, Activity

In the box with the square, draw something that is good. In the box with the heart, draw something that is loving. In the box with the triangle, draw something that is fun. In the box with the circle, draw something that is helpful.

GOOD	LOVING
FUN	HELPFUL

TRINITY: Lesson 1, Scripture Exploration

"THEN GOD SAID, 'LET US MAKE MAN IN OUR IMAGE, AFTER OUR LIKENESS.'"

—GENESIS 1:26A

TRINITY: Lesson 2, Focus Activity

What is God like? Think of words you know that describe what God is like. For example, God is good, loving, fun, and helpful. In the box below, draw examples of things that remind you of what God is like.

TRINITY: Lesson 2, Activity

While you create each three-in-one picture, describe each person of the Trinity out loud. For example, while I draw three beautiful flowers, I am thinking about how beautiful God is. To help myself remember that all three persons of the Trinity are beautiful, out loud I can say, "God the Father is beautiful, God the Son is beautiful, and God the Holy Spirit is beautiful. All three persons are beautiful."

EXAMPLE:

BEAUTIFUL

HAPPY

HELPFUL

LOVING

TRINITY: Lesson 2, Scripture Exploration

Review the verse you started to explore last week.

"THEN GOD SAID, 'LET US MAKE MAN IN OUR IMAGE, AFTER OUR LIKENESS.'"

—GENESIS 1:26A

TRINITY: Lesson 3, Focus Activity

Sketch a fun memory of a time you got to be with a good friend.

TRINITY: Lesson 3, Activity

God is a Friend, and God has Friends.

God made me a friend, and God gives me friends.

In the boxes below, sketch yourself, your friend, and a way the Holy Spirit helps you to love your friend (something you do or say to your friend to show them you love them).

ME	MY FRIEND

SOMETHING THE HOLY SPIRIT HELPS ME DO TO LOVE MY FRIEND:

TRINITY: Lesson 3, Scripture Exploration

"THE FATHER LOVES THE SON AND HAS GIVEN ALL THINGS INTO HIS HAND."

—JOHN 3:35

TRINITY: Lesson 4, Focus Activity

God made us like him and wants us to be friends with him and with other people. Think of some of the friends that God has given you (for example, brothers and sisters, and other boys and girls). Sketch some of your friends in the box below.

TRINITY: Lesson 4, Activity

Below, draw a quick sketch of how someone feels the more they see Jesus changing their heart.

TRINITY: Lesson 4, Scripture Exploration

Review the verse you started to explore last week.

"THE FATHER LOVES THE SON AND HAS GIVEN ALL THINGS INTO HIS HAND."

—JOHN 3:35

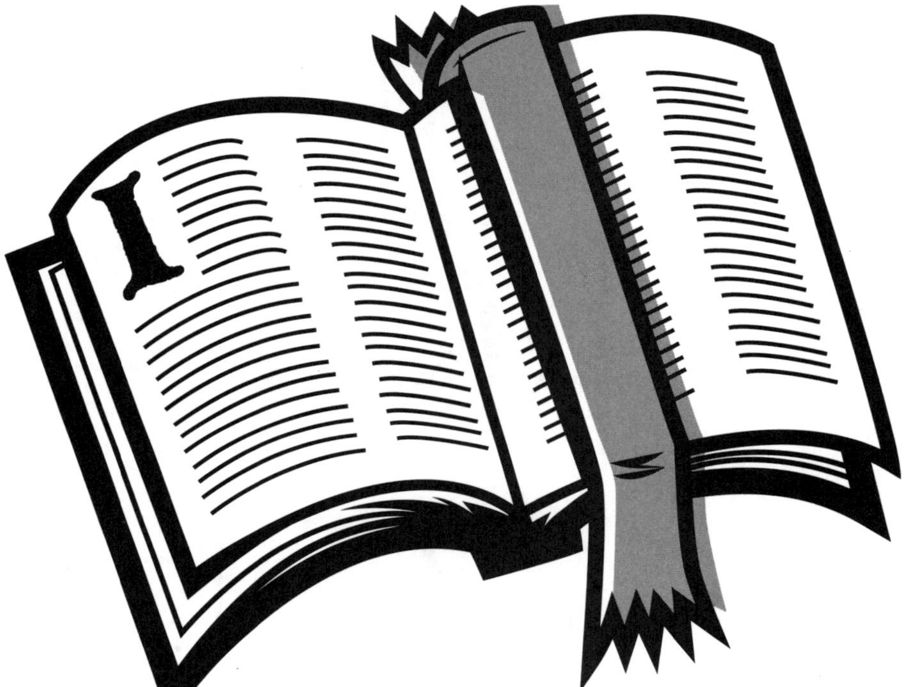

REVELATION: Lesson 1, Focus Activity

God made all of creation. Creation includes people, places, plants, animals, and things. God speaks through creation, and he shows us who he is through the things he has made in the world. In the box below, sketch examples of things God made.

REVELATION: Lesson 1, Activity

God speaks through creation.

God shows us who he is through the things he has made in the world.

In each box, draw something that God made that tells you about who he is.

REVELATION: Lesson 1, Scripture Exploration

"THE HEAVENS DECLARE THE GLORY OF GOD, AND THE SKY ABOVE PROCLAIMS HIS HANDIWORK."

—PSALM 19:1

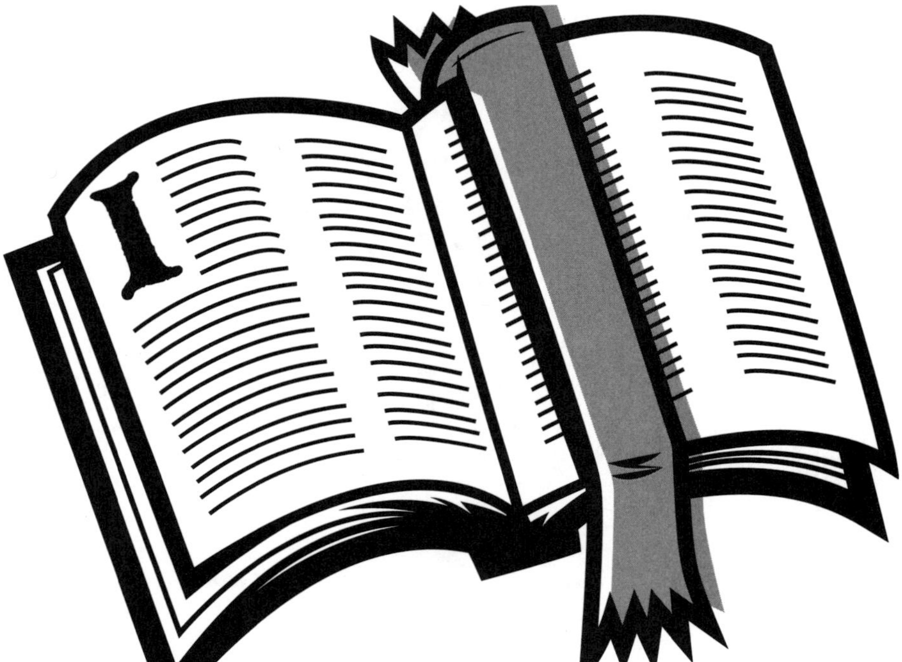

REVELATION: Lesson 2, Focus Activity

Sketch a time when you knew the right thing to do.

REVELATION: Lesson 2, Activity

Draw a quick sketch of a time when your conscience told you what was wrong.

Who made your conscience?

REVELATION: Lesson 2, Scripture Exploration

Review the verse you started to explore last week.

"THE HEAVENS DECLARE THE GLORY OF GOD, AND THE SKY ABOVE PROCLAIMS HIS HANDIWORK."

—PSALM 19:1

REVELATION: Lesson 3, Focus Activity

Think of where and how you learn about God. Look at the following pictures. Color the pictures that show ways or people that help you learn about God. Ask yourself, "Does ____ help me learn about God?"

REVELATION: Lesson 3, Activity

Does God want just some people to know about himself? Or everyone? (Circle answer.)

Now, in the box below, draw a quick sketch showing what you know about God's Big Story (that he tells everyone about!).

REVELATION: Lesson 3, Scripture Exploration

"ALL
SCRIPTURE
IS BREATHED
OUT BY GOD."

—2 TIMOTHY 3:16A

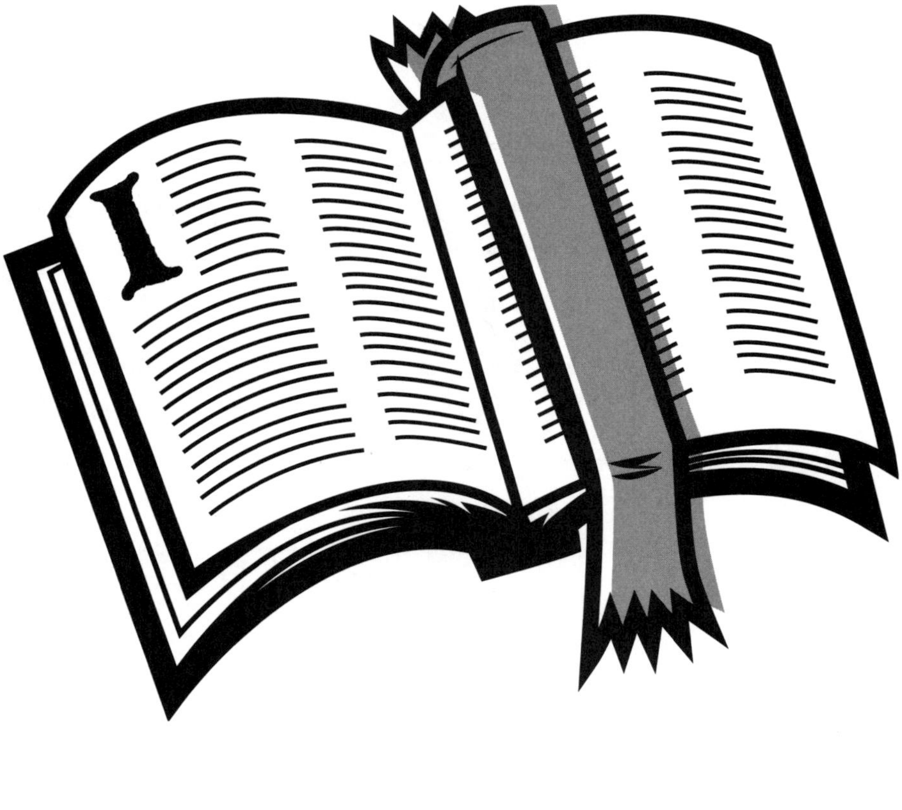

REVELATION: Lesson 4, Focus Activity

Brainstorm people you know who love Jesus.

Sketch at least two of these people in the box provided.

How do you know they love Jesus?

REVELATION: Lesson 4, Activity

God wants to speak to us all the time.

God speaks to us through Scripture (the Bible) and by speaking to our hearts.

Color the pictures of times when God wants to speak to you.

WHEN I FEEL SAD

WHEN I FEEL HAPPY

WHEN I AM MAD

WHEN SOMETHING IS EASY FOR ME

WHEN SOMETHING IS HARD FOR ME

WHEN I AM HAVING FUN

REVELATION: Lesson 4, Scripture Exploration

Review the verse you started to explore last week.

"ALL SCRIPTURE IS BREATHED OUT BY GOD."

—2 TIMOTHY 3:16A

CREATION: Lesson 1, Focus Activity

Sketch a few of your favorites . . .

MY FAVORITE FOOD	MY FAVORITE SPORT
MY FAVORITE GAME TO PLAY WITH MY FRIENDS	MY FAVORITE PLACE TO GO WITH MY FAMILY

Who made all of your favorites?

CREATION: Lesson 1, Activity

What are some things God created that you really love?
Sketch the first three things that come to mind in the boxes below.

CREATION: Lesson 1, Scripture Exploration

"IN THE BEGINNING, GOD CREATED THE HEAVENS AND THE EARTH."

—GENESIS 1:1

CREATION: Lesson 2, Focus Activity

Who takes care of you at home? How do they take care of you? In each box below, sketch an example of a way that they take care of you.

CREATION: Lesson 2, Activity

Stop and think about God's Big Story. In the boxes below, sketch three snapshots of God's Big Story: (1) the start of the Story, (2) the part where Jesus lives out the Rescue Plan, and (3) the part of God's Story you are living right now!

●

♥

▲

CREATION: Lesson 2, Scripture Exploration

Review the verse you started to explore last week.

"IN THE

BEGINNING,

GOD CREATED

THE HEAVENS

AND THE

EARTH."

—GENESIS 1:1

CREATION: Lesson 3, Focus Activity

Circle and color some of God's gifts that you are thankful for.

CREATION: Lesson 3, Activity

I CAN THANK GOD FOR ...

CREATION: Lesson 3, Scripture Exploration

"HOLY, HOLY, HOLY IS THE LORD OF HOSTS; THE WHOLE EARTH IS FULL OF HIS GLORY!"

—ISAIAH 6:3B

CREATION: Lesson 4, Focus Activity

Think of a time when you have said "Thank you" for something. It could be for a gift someone gave you, or for something that someone did for you.

Draw what you were thankful for in the box below.

CREATION: Lesson 4, Activity

We can glorify God by thanking him for the gifts he gives us.

Think of a time you or someone you know thanked God for one of his gifts. How did you feel? Below, sketch a picture of what you feel like when you thank God. (Show the feeling on the face of your drawing.)

CREATION: Lesson 4, Scripture Exploration

Review the verse you started to explore last week.

"HOLY, HOLY,
HOLY IS THE
LORD OF
HOSTS; THE
WHOLE EARTH
IS FULL OF
HIS GLORY!"

—ISAIAH 6:3B

IMAGE: Lesson 1, Focus Activity

Pretend that the frame below is a mirror. What do you see when you look in a mirror?

Draw what you see in the frame below.

IMAGE: Lesson 1, Activity

Circle and color the things that are made in the image of God. Cross out the things that are not made in the image of God.

IMAGE: Lesson 1, Scripture Exploration

"SO GOD CREATED MAN IN HIS OWN IMAGE."

—GENESIS 1:27A

IMAGE: Lesson 2, Focus Activity

Draw a person. All people are made in the image of God.

Draw an animal, or a plant, or a thing. These are not made in the image of God. Only people are made in the image of God.

IMAGE: Lesson 2, Activity

Circle the pictures that show some things that only people can do that other things in creation cannot.

TALK TO GOD

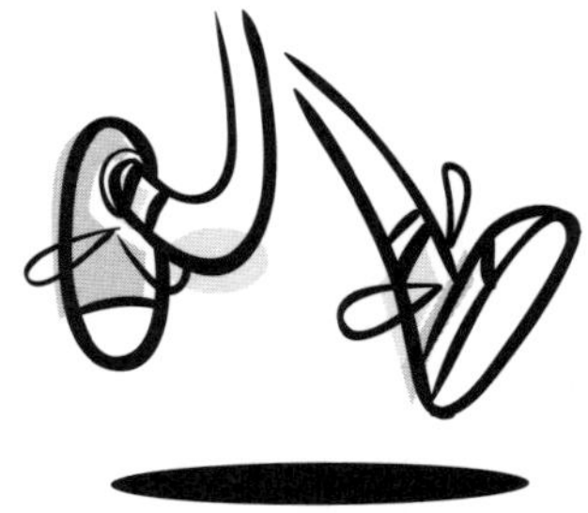

RUN

WORSHIP

EAT

PAINT

HAVE A RELATIONSHIP WITH GOD

IMAGE: Lesson 2, Scripture Exploration

Review the verse you started to explore last week.

"SO GOD CREATED MAN IN HIS OWN IMAGE."

—GENESIS 1:27A

IMAGE: Lesson 3, Focus Activity

Circle the pairs that are a little like each other.

Cross out the pairs that are not.

You are made in God's image.

You have qualities that are a little like God's.

IMAGE: Lesson 3, Activity

When we love Jesus, we respond by obeying him and acting out our qualities that are a little like his.

In each box, draw a picture of something you do that shows you are a little like God.

THE HOLY SPIRIT HELPS ME TO...

IMAGE: Lesson 3, Scripture Exploration

"MY FLESH AND MY HEART MAY FAIL, BUT GOD IS THE STRENGTH OF MY HEART AND MY PORTION FOREVER."

—PSALM 73:26

IMAGE: Lesson 4, Focus Activity

Brainstorm things that are alike.

In each box below, draw a pair of things that are similar.

IMAGE: Lesson 4, Activity

One of the things I do that is a little like what God does is pray. Praying is a little like what God does because God the Father, God the Son, and God the Holy Spirit are always talking to each other and serving each other.

Sketch a quick picture of you or someone you know praying.

IMAGE: Lesson 4, Scripture Exploration

Review the verse you started to explore last week.

"MY FLESH AND
MY HEART MAY
FAIL, BUT GOD IS
THE STRENGTH
OF MY HEART
AND MY PORTION
FOREVER."

—PSALM 73:26

FALL: Lesson 1, Focus Activity

Are there problems in the world? Stop and sketch or write about at least two problems you have seen or heard of.

FALL: Lesson 1, Activity

Imagine that you are watching a movie of the fall, and the movie pauses at the moment when Adam and Eve realize what they have done. Draw a picture of what you see, and feel free to add words.

FALL: Lesson 1, Scripture Exploration

"SIN CAME INTO THE WORLD THROUGH ONE MAN."

—ROMANS 5:12A

FALL: Lesson 2, Focus Activity

Take a moment to remember what you learned last week about when Adam and Eve disobeyed God. Who was there? What happened?

Sketch a picture of what happened in the box below.

FALL: Lesson 2, Activity

We can sin by doing, and we can also sin by not doing.

- In the top box, sketch a time you have done something God didn't want you to do.
- In the bottom box, sketch a time when you didn't do something God wanted you to do.

SOMETIMES I SIN BY DOING THE WRONG THING:

SOMETIMES I SIN BY NOT DOING THE RIGHT THING:

FALL: Lesson 2, Scripture Exploration

Review the verse you started to explore last week.

"SIN CAME INTO THE WORLD THROUGH ONE MAN."

—ROMANS 5:12A

FALL: Lesson 3, Focus Activity

Sketch a picture of what you've learned so far about the fall. Who was involved? What happened?

FALL: Lesson 3, Activity

Circle and color the people who sin. Cross out the people who do not sin.

FALL: Lesson 3, Scripture Exploration

"FOR AS IN ADAM ALL DIE, SO ALSO IN CHRIST SHALL ALL BE MADE ALIVE."

—I CORINTHIANS 15:22

FALL: Lesson 4, Focus Activity

Who sins? Stop and think about people you know who sin. (Hint: *everyone sins*, including you!) In the box below, sketch yourself and at least one other person who sins.

FALL: Lesson 4, Activity

Before they left the garden, God gave a promise to Adam and Eve. Draw a picture of what God promised would happen at just the right time.

How does God's promise connect to you?

FALL: Lesson 4, Scripture Exploration

Review the verse you started to explore last week.

"FOR AS IN ADAM ALL DIE, SO ALSO IN CHRIST SHALL ALL BE MADE ALIVE."

—I CORINTHIANS 15:22

COVENANT: Lesson 1, Focus Activity

Draw a picture of a time you made a promise or someone made a promise to you.

Do people always keep their promises?

COVENANT: Lesson 1, Activity

Circle and color all the people who need to be rescued by Jesus.

Everyone in the world needs Jesus all of the time.

COVENANT: Lesson 1, Scripture Exploration

"BEHOLD, I ESTABLISH MY COVENANT WITH YOU AND YOUR OFFSPRING AFTER YOU."

—GENESIS 9:9

COVENANT: Lesson 2, Focus Activity

Draw a picture of a time you broke a promise, or someone broke a promise they made to you.

COVENANT: Lesson 2, Activity

Sketch the reminder that God created in the sky to tell us about his Forever Promise.

COVENANT: Lesson 2, Scripture Exploration

Review the verse you started to explore last week.

"BEHOLD, I ESTABLISH MY COVENANT WITH YOU AND YOUR OFFSPRING AFTER YOU."

—GENESIS 9:9

COVENANT: Lesson 3, Focus Activity

Sketch one of God's promises that you know about and add words if you'd like. (Feel free to draw one of the covenants we learned about last week: God's promise to Noah and his promise to the whole world through Jesus.)

COVENANT: Lesson 3, Activity

Circle and color the people that God wants to hear about his Forever Promise.

COVENANT: Lesson 3, Scripture Exploration

"AND I WILL ESTABLISH MY COVENANT BETWEEN ME AND YOU AND YOUR OFFSPRING AFTER YOU."

—GENESIS 17:7A

COVENANT: Lesson 4, Focus Activity

Think of a time when you had to wait for something. You were expecting something, but it didn't happen right away.

Draw what happened in the box below.

COVENANT: Lesson 4, Activity

Sketch what you know about God's promise to Abraham.

COVENANT: Lesson 4, Scripture Exploration

Review the verse you started to explore last week.

"AND I WILL
ESTABLISH
MY COVENANT
BETWEEN
ME AND YOU
AND YOUR
OFFSPRING
AFTER YOU."

—GENESIS 17:7A

INCARNATION: Lesson 1, Focus Activity

Jesus the Son was born on the earth as a baby, just like every other person on the earth. In the box below, sketch a picture of Jesus as a baby.

INCARNATION: Lesson 1, Activity

Jesus is eternal. This means that Jesus has always existed in the past, exists now, and will continue to exist forever. Circle and color the times when Jesus has existed. Hint: *always!*

INCARNATION: Lesson 1, Scripture Exploration

"AND THE WORD BECAME FLESH AND DWELT AMONG US."

—JOHN 1:14A

INCARNATION: Lesson 2, Focus Activity

You are human. Your friends are human. Your teacher is human. Your mom and dad are human. Stop and think—what are some things that everyone needs to do? What are some feelings that everyone has? In the box below, sketch examples of things that are true about everyone.

INCARNATION: Lesson 2, Activity

Earlier, you thought about things that every human does or experiences. Now, since Jesus was fully man, let's think about some of the things he did and experienced while he lived on the earth. Circle and color everything Jesus did. Cross out the things he did not do.

INCARNATION: Lesson 2, Scripture Exploration

Review the verse you started to explore last week.

"AND THE WORD BECAME FLESH AND DWELT AMONG US."

—JOHN 1:14A

INCARNATION: Lesson 3, Focus Activity

Think of people or things that are powerful. Things that are powerful are really, really strong. Draw as many powerful things as you can in the box below.

INCARNATION: Lesson 3, Activity

Each picture below is an example from the Bible of something Jesus did during his life on this earth as both God and man that shows that he is powerful. Describe each picture out loud. Then, after you describe the picture, color it in.

INCARNATION: Lesson 3, Scripture Exploration

JESUS "IN EVERY RESPECT HAS BEEN TEMPTED AS WE ARE, YET WITHOUT SIN."

—HEBREWS 4:15B

INCARNATION: Lesson 4, Focus Activity

Have you ever done something loving? Have you seen someone else do something loving? In the box below, draw at least one example of someone doing something loving.

Who did the most loving thing anyone has ever done? What did he do? Why?

INCARNATION: Lesson 4, Activity

When we love Jesus and believe that he is the Savior from sin, he changes our hearts and our lives so that we become more and more like him. We cannot be patient or loving on our own, but through the Holy Spirit, Jesus helps us to become more patient and more loving as we grow in faith.

- In the box with the circle, draw an example of a time when you were patient.
- In the box with the square, draw an example of a time when you were loving.

PATIENT

LOVING

Thank Jesus that he helps you to be patient and loving!

INCARNATION: Lesson 4, Scripture Exploration

Review the verse you started to explore last week.

JESUS "IN EVERY RESPECT HAS BEEN TEMPTED AS WE ARE, YET WITHOUT SIN."

—HEBREWS 4:15B

INRI

CROSS: Lesson 1, Focus Activity

In the boxes provided, sketch what you know about Jesus' part in living out God's Rescue Plan as both God and man. Jesus knew about the plan from before the beginning, and agreed to live it out.

JESUS COMES:

JESUS DIES:

JESUS LIVES:

CROSS: Lesson 1, Activity

Listen to the story of the cross from *The Jesus Storybook Bible*. While you listen, sketch a picture of the scene that you are hearing about.

CROSS: Lesson 1, Scripture Exploration

"FOR OUR SAKE HE MADE HIM TO BE SIN WHO KNEW NO SIN."

—2 CORINTHIANS 5:21A

INRI

CROSS: Lesson 2, Focus Activity

Think of a time you or someone you know got hurt. In the box below, tell what happened using words or pictures.

CROSS: Lesson 2, Activity

How did Jesus suffer? Brainstorm some of the ways he was hurt. Then, in the space provided, sketch a picture of how Jesus must have been feeling while he was being hurt so badly.

CROSS: Lesson 2, Scripture Exploration

Review the verse you started to explore last week.

"FOR OUR SAKE HE MADE HIM TO BE SIN WHO KNEW NO SIN."

—2 CORINTHIANS 5:21A

INRI

CROSS: Lesson 3, Focus Activity

Sketch a picture showing what you know about the cross. Who was there? What was happening? Where did it happen? Include as many details as you can in your picture.

CROSS: Lesson 3, Activity

Color the picture of Jesus' death on the cross.

While you color, discuss how Jesus died and why he died.

CROSS: Lesson 3, Scripture Exploration

"AND BEING FOUND IN HUMAN FORM, HE HUMBLED HIMSELF BY BECOMING OBEDIENT TO THE POINT OF DEATH, EVEN DEATH ON A CROSS."

—PHILIPPIANS 2:8

INRI

CROSS: Lesson 4, Focus Activity

Think of a time when you have paid for something.
What did you pay for? How did you pay for it?

Draw or describe your experience in the box below.

Jesus also paid for something.

What did he pay for? How did he pay?

CROSS: Lesson 4, Activity

How does it make you feel to think about how Jesus died? How does it make you feel to know *why* he died?

Sketch how you feel in each box.

When I think about how Jesus died, I feel . . .

When I think about why Jesus died, I feel . . .

CROSS: Lesson 4, Scripture Exploration

Review the verse you started to explore last week.

"AND BEING FOUND IN HUMAN FORM, HE HUMBLED HIMSELF BY BECOMING OBEDIENT TO THE POINT OF DEATH, EVEN DEATH ON A CROSS."

—PHILIPPIANS 2:8

RESURRECTION: Lesson 1, Focus Activity

In the box below, sketch a picture showing what you know about the cross.

RESURRECTION: Lesson 1, Activity

Draw pictures showing the sequence of some of the events of the resurrection. If you need help getting ideas, check out an illustrated children's Bible like *The Jesus Storybook Bible*, *The Big Picture Story Bible*, or *The Gospel Story Bible*.

Draw Jesus appearing to the disciples for the first time in his new body.

Draw something Jesus did while he was on the earth in his better-than-before body.

Draw Jesus rising up to heaven.

RESURRECTION: Lesson 1, Scripture Exploration

"'"WHOEVER BELIEVES IN ME, THOUGH HE DIE, YET SHALL HE LIVE.'"

—JOHN 11:25B

RESURRECTION: Lesson 2, Focus Activity

Think of a time you were surprised by something. You expected one thing to happen, but something different happened instead. In the box below, tell what happened using words or pictures.

How do you think Jesus' friends felt when they saw that he was alive again?

RESURRECTION: Lesson 2, Activity

When Jesus rose from the dead, he did many things in his better-than-before body that helped show that he was really alive again. Color and discuss the examples below.

RESURRECTION: Lesson 2, Scripture Exploration

Review the verse you started to explore last week.

"'WHOEVER BELIEVES IN ME, THOUGH HE DIE, YET SHALL HE LIVE.'"

—JOHN 11:25B

RESURRECTION: Lesson 3, Focus Activity

Think of a time when something changed you: maybe you liked something for the first time, or thought of something in a different way. Draw that time in the box below.

RESURRECTION: Lesson 3, Activity

Color and discuss the pictures of Peter before and after the resurrection. Consider:

- Is Peter worshiping Jesus in this picture?
- Is Peter telling others about Jesus?

Before the resurrection: On the day Jesus died, Peter denied Jesus three times. He acted like he didn't even know him!

After the resurrection: Peter preached to thousands of people. God changed their hearts so they believed in Jesus as the Savior from sin and received the Holy Spirit.

RESURRECTION: Lesson 3, Scripture Exploration

"AND HE WHO WAS SEATED ON THE THRONE SAID, 'BEHOLD, I AM MAKING ALL THINGS NEW.'"

—REVELATION 21:5A

RESURRECTION: Lesson 4, Focus Activity

Think of a time something or someone you know changed: they started out one way, then became another way. After they changed, they were not the same.

In the boxes below, draw what they were like before and after.

BEFORE:

AFTER:

RESURRECTION: Lesson 4, Activity

What an amazing thing! Just like Jesus' better-than-before body was in perfect health, our bodies will be too. When Jesus returns, everyone who believes will have bodies that never go through pain or get hurt or die.

In the box below, sketch what you think your better-than-before body in Jesus' brand-new world might look like if you have believed in Jesus as the Savior from sin.

RESURRECTION: Lesson 4, Scripture Exploration

Review the verse you started to explore last week.

"AND HE WHO WAS SEATED ON THE THRONE SAID, 'BEHOLD, I AM MAKING ALL THINGS NEW.'"

—REVELATION 21:5A

CHURCH: Lesson 1, Focus Activity

In the box below, draw a picture of the church.

CHURCH: Lesson 1, Activity

Circle and color the pictures of things that people in the local church do together.

CHURCH: Lesson 1, Scripture Exploration

"CHRIST LOVED THE CHURCH AND GAVE HIMSELF UP FOR HER."

—EPHESIANS 5:25B

CHURCH: Lesson 2, Focus Activity

The church is all people who believe in Jesus as the Savior from sin. Who do you know that is part of the church? Are you part of the church?

In the box below, draw at least one person you know who is part of the church.

CHURCH: Lesson 2, Activity

Is the church a building? In the box below, draw a picture of what you think the church looks like now.

CHURCH: Lesson 2, Scripture Exploration

Review the verse you started to explore last week.

"CHRIST LOVED THE CHURCH AND GAVE HIMSELF UP FOR HER."

—EPHESIANS 5:25B

CHURCH: Lesson 3, Focus Activity

God's people do lots of things together. In the box, sketch as many examples of things you do with God's people as you can think of. You can include things you do at the church building, or things you do with God's people throughout the week.

You do lots of things with God's people, but what do you think Jesus' special mission for the church is? Today we'll find out . . .

CHURCH: Lesson 3, Activity

Jesus wants people to believe in him and be part of his special mission today. Look at the pictures and ask yourself, "Is this something someone who loves Jesus could do to carry out Jesus' special mission to tell people about him?" If it is, circle and color the picture. If it isn't, cross it out.

CHURCH: Lesson 3, Scripture Exploration

"GO THEREFORE AND MAKE DISCIPLES OF ALL NATIONS."

—MATTHEW 28:19A

CHURCH: Lesson 4, Focus Activity

What is the special mission that Jesus gave the church? Tell about the mission in the space below using words or pictures.

CHURCH: Lesson 4, Activity

What are some of the things God's people did in the New Testament to carry out Jesus' special mission? Sketch all the examples that you can think of in the box below.

CHURCH: Lesson 4, Scripture Exploration

Review the verse you started to explore last week.

"GO THEREFORE AND MAKE DISCIPLES OF ALL NATIONS."

—MATTHEW 28:19A

WORSHIP: Lesson 1, Focus Activity

Think of the word "worship." What do you picture when you think of the word? Sketch it in the space below.

WORSHIP: Lesson 1, Activity

In the Bible, God gives us many examples of times when his people were worshiping him. He also gives examples of times his people worshiped someone or something other than him. Color and discuss the pictures. Circle the examples of worshiping God. Cross out the examples of worshiping someone or something else.

THE FALL (EVE BELIEVES THE SERPENT'S LIE)

GOD'S PEOPLE WORSHIP THE GOLDEN CALF

PETER PREACHES ABOUT JESUS TO THOUSANDS OF PEOPLE

WORSHIP: Lesson 1, Scripture Exploration

"'TRUE WORSHIPERS WILL WORSHIP THE FATHER IN SPIRIT AND TRUTH.'"

—JOHN 4:23B

WORSHIP: Lesson 2, Focus Activity

Who worships? Do you worship? Do other people you know worship? (Hint: every person worships all the time!) In the box below, draw at least three people you know who worship.

WORSHIP: Lesson 2, Activity

Color and discuss examples of things that God's people sometimes do together at the church building to worship Jesus. Remember that these things are only worship if in your heart you are loving Jesus and living for him while you do them.

WORSHIP: Lesson 2, Scripture Exploration

Review the verse you started to explore last week.

"'TRUE WORSHIPERS WILL WORSHIP THE FATHER IN SPIRIT AND TRUTH.'"

—JOHN 4:23B

WORSHIP: Lesson 3, Focus Activity

Many things change. They start out one way, then become another way. Something about them is new or different. As you color each picture, change at least one thing about it.

Did you know that your heart can change, too? Did you know that you can become new on the inside? Today we'll talk about how . . .

WORSHIP: Lesson 3, Activity

When Jesus changes your heart to love him, he changes who or what you really love and live for, then bit by bit he changes your whole life. In each box, listen to how the person was acting before they met Jesus and believed in him as the Savior from sin. Then, sketch how you think their actions might change in response to who Jesus is.

Before: A boy does not want to share his toys with his sister.

After:

Before: A girl does not obey her mother's direction that it is bedtime.

After:

Before: A man spends all his money on nice things for himself.

After:

Before: A woman takes a bracelet from her friend without asking.

After:

WORSHIP: Lesson 3, Scripture Exploration

"THEREFORE,
IF ANYONE IS IN
CHRIST, HE IS A NEW
CREATION. THE OLD
HAS PASSED AWAY;
BEHOLD, THE NEW
HAS COME."

—2 CORINTHIANS 5:17

WORSHIP: Lesson 4, Focus Activity

Every person worships all of the time. This means that you are worshiping someone or something in the morning, in the afternoon, and in the evening—all of the time! In the boxes below, sketch the times of day when you are worshiping.

In the morning . . .

In the afternoon . . .

In the evening . . .

WORSHIP: Lesson 4, Activity

Jesus changed Saul's heart to love and live for him (to worship him!), then changed everything in Saul's life, from his name to the things that he wanted to do. In the boxes below, sketch Saul's life before and after he believed in Jesus.

BEFORE:

AFTER:

WORSHIP: Lesson 4, Scripture Exploration

Review the verse you started to explore last week.

"THEREFORE,
IF ANYONE IS IN
CHRIST, HE IS A NEW
CREATION. THE OLD
HAS PASSED AWAY;
BEHOLD, THE NEW
HAS COME."

—2 CORINTHIANS 5:17

STEWARDSHIP: Lesson 1, Focus Activity

God gives us many gifts to enjoy, take care of, and share with others. What are some of your favorite things that you have? Draw at least three things in the box below.

STEWARDSHIP: Lesson 1, Activity

Circle and color pictures that show kids stewarding things well. Cross out pictures that show kids not stewarding well.

STEWARDSHIP: Lesson 1, Scripture Exploration

"AS EACH HAS RECEIVED A GIFT, USE IT TO SERVE ONE ANOTHER, AS GOOD STEWARDS OF GOD'S VARIED GRACE."

—1 PETER 4:10

STEWARDSHIP: Lesson 2, Focus Activity

Think of a time you saw someone take extra special care of something. They were stewarding it by taking care of it well. Sketch that time in the box below.

STEWARDSHIP: Lesson 2, Activity

What are some of the things God has given you to take care of? Sketch one example in each box below.

STEWARDSHIP: Lesson 2, Scripture Exploration

Review the verse you started to explore last week.

"AS EACH HAS
RECEIVED A GIFT,
USE IT TO SERVE
ONE ANOTHER, AS
GOOD STEWARDS
OF GOD'S VARIED
GRACE."

—I PETER 4:10

STEWARDSHIP: Lesson 3, Focus Activity

What are some of your favorite things that you like to do with your time? Draw at least three examples in the box below.

STEWARDSHIP: Lesson 3, Activity

How could you steward your time well? In the heart below, sketch a picture of you using your time well.

(The picture is in a heart because if you are stewarding your time to worship God, you are doing it because you really, really love him and live for him.)

STEWARDSHIP: Lesson 3, Scripture Exploration

"'HE HAS DISTRIBUTED FREELY, HE HAS GIVEN TO THE POOR; HIS RIGHTEOUSNESS ENDURES FOREVER.'"

—2 CORINTHIANS 9:9B

STEWARDSHIP: Lesson 4, Focus Activity

What is something that you are good at?

Sketch or describe your talent in the box below.

STEWARDSHIP: Lesson 4, Activity

Circle and color examples of treasure that you can share with others. Remember that you are worshiping if you are sharing in response to who Jesus is and what he has shared with you. Cross out things that are not examples of treasure.

STEWARDSHIP: Lesson 4, Scripture Exploration

Review the verse you started to explore last week.

"'''HE HAS DISTRIBUTED FREELY, HE HAS GIVEN TO THE POOR; HIS RIGHTEOUSNESS ENDURES FOREVER.'''

—2 CORINTHIANS 9:9B

KINGDOM: Lesson 1, Focus Activity

In the box below, sketch a picture of what you think a king looks like.

Do you know who the King of kings is? Today we'll find out . . .

KINGDOM: Lesson 1, Activity

Jesus is the King of kings! Color the picture of King Jesus below. While you color, discuss what you know about Jesus the King.

KINGDOM: Lesson 1, Scripture Exploration

"YOUR KINGDOM COME, YOUR WILL BE DONE, ON EARTH AS IT IS IN HEAVEN."

—MATTHEW 6:10

KINGDOM: Lesson 2, Focus Activity

Imagine that you wake up tomorrow and the city where you live has no sin and no problems. What would your city be like?

Draw what you think it would be like in the box below.

KINGDOM: Lesson 2, Activity

What will the new earth be like? Will it be a good Forever Home? Sketch a picture of what you think the new earth will look like in the box below.

KINGDOM: Lesson 2, Scripture Exploration

Review the verse you started to explore last week.

"“YOUR KINGDOM COME, YOUR WILL BE DONE, ON EARTH AS IT IS IN HEAVEN.”"

—MATTHEW 6:10

KINGDOM: Lesson 3, Focus Activity

In the space below, sketch a picture showing what you know about Jesus' Forever Kingdom.

KINGDOM: Lesson 3, Activity

Draw a picture of someone you know who loves Jesus. Did you know that Jesus' kingdom has started right there in their heart?

KINGDOM: Lesson 3, Scripture Exploration

"“HE WILL WIPE AWAY EVERY TEAR FROM THEIR EYES, AND DEATH SHALL BE NO MORE.’”

—REVELATION 21:4A

KINGDOM: Lesson 4, Focus Activity

Jesus' kingdom has already begun in the hearts of people who believe in him as the Savior from sin. In the box below, sketch at least one person you know who is part of Jesus' Forever Kingdom.

KINGDOM: Lesson 4, Activity

We know that Jesus' kingdom is already and not yet. Look at each picture and ask yourself, "Has this part of Jesus' kingdom arrived already, or not yet?" Next to each picture, write "A" for already or "N" for not yet.

KINGDOM: Lesson 4, Scripture Exploration

Review the verse you started to explore last week.

"HE WILL WIPE AWAY EVERY TEAR FROM THEIR EYES, AND DEATH SHALL BE NO MORE."

—REVELATION 21:4A